42 Strategies to Market Your Book:

An Author's Guide

SHARI W. QUINN, MBA

SHARI W. QUINN

OTHER BOOKS
BY SHARI W. QUINN

Disloyalty

SHARI W. QUINN

Published by Shari Quinn Publishing

FIRST EDITION

Available on Kindle and other retail outlets

To order additional copies of this title, contact your favorite bookstore or visit www.shariquinn.com or email: info@shariquinn.com

Cover Design by Shari W. Quinn
Cover Image © Andrey Kuzmin, 2014
Used under license from Shuterstock.com

Edited by Shari W. Quinn

Interior Design by Shari W. Quinn

Printed in the United States of America
CreateSpace, Charleston, SC

ISBN: 0692347747
ISBN-13: 978-0692347744

SHARI W. QUINN

.

To my children:
Sharia, Ruffus "Pop," and Malik

Everything I do, I do it for you. In everything you do, do your best.

Love,
Mom

SHARI W. QUINN

Contents

SHARI W. QUINN

42 Strategies to Market

Your Book:

An Author's Guide

SHARI W. QUINN

Acknowledgements

I appreciate all the wonderful people who supported me along the journey, and for making *Disloyalty* a best-seller. It's an amazing feeling to have your first book fly off the bookshelves. Your continuous support motivated me to write this second book.

I would also like to thank a friend that I've known for more than 10 years who helped me see life through a clearer lens rather than rose-colored lenses with distorted views.

"It is true that you don't know what you have until it's gone, and it's also true that you don't know what you were missing until it arrives." – Unknown

I'm on my way to a much better me and am walking in to greatness!

Thank you,
xoxo

SHARI W. QUINN

Prelude

After the soaring-high volume sales of my best-selling novel, *Disloyalty,* many authors, readers and interviewers asked how I created such a buzz and social media phenomenon about my new book. Other authors have also asked about my marketing and promotion strategies, and selling a highly sought after book. With an effective strategic and well-thought out comprehensive marketing plan, my book practically sold itself. It was nice to just sit back, get exposure and collect royalties from many book stores and distribution channels around the world.

My suggested strategies are inexpensive, cost-effective, and in many cases – free. Because I received such great exposure and success with my first book, I wanted to share with other authors the keys to marketing success. Most authors are fantastic writers, however, they are not marketing experts. I was fortunate enough to have a MBA and an undergraduate degree, both with a marketing concentration. My formal education and field experience helped develop me as a marketing strategist at heart so developing and implementing effective marketing ideas is my forte and second nature. Further, I strongly believe in sharing knowledge, as the old adage says, "to whom much is given, much is required," and I am delighted to share best practices with other authors.

By implementing these proven strategies, you can hopefully share the same success with your book and future projects as I have with mine. Let this book serve as your blueprint to outlining effective and efficient marketing plans, initiatives and practices.

The list of marketing strategies is not listed in an order of importance although I attempted to rearrange the order to list them by the most crucial. I truly hope these strategies add value and success to your project. You should be proud of your accomplishment and allows others to be proud of your too; getting the word out about your book will help accomplish this goal.

Please feel free to provide your feedback with others on Twitter: @shariquinn2 using the hashtag #42WaysToMarket or on my Official Facebook page, Shari Quinn. You are welcome to post your views on Amazon, or send a message via shariquinn2.com.

Best of luck to you and your book.

SHARI W. QUINN

#1 Extend Your Distribution

List your book with as many book distribution channels as possible for increased exposure and availability. You can list with publishing sites such as such as Kindle, Nook, iBooks, Amazon, Barnes & Noble, CreateSpace, and with as many book stores as possible. Listing your book with CreateSpace allows your book to have access to an extended distribution service as well as reach domestic and international markets you would not otherwise have reached. Many independent publishers companies have the capabilities to list your book for you.

My best-selling novel, *Disloyalty*, is currently sold in more than seven countries including the United States, the UK, France, Denmark, China, Japan and even Australia. Readers in various markets across the world are purchasing and reading my creative work, as a direct result of my expansion and intense marketing strategies. Equally important, an increase in distribution channels equates to increased sales and royalties.

#2 Build a Team

Unless you are unemployed or retired, you do not have enough time to manage the book promotions yourself. I suggest creating a team of unpaid interns to help support the process. You can contact the Career Services department at one of the local colleges in your area. I would also suggest including junior students as your interns to give them the opportunity to work with you over the next two years or on your other book projects as well before they graduate. Students will be delighted to have the opportunity and experience. Junior and senior college students are generally ambitious and hungry for practical hands-on experience prior to entering the workforce. The internship experience will help them apply the concepts and theories learned in the classroom to the real-world environment, and ultimately build their will resume. You can also partner with the Career Services department or the student's academic advisor to allow the student to receive college credit toward their degree for their experience. Even though it's a unpaid internship, the student will be very happy with the experience, and a small token of appreciation such as meal card, gas card or small stipend.

If you decide to get interns, create a team of two to four students to include the following three majors: English/Communications, Marketing and possibly Computer Science. The English major student can assist you with writing small articles, press releases for publications and other content related to your book. The marketing student is your strategist to develop and implement a solid marketing plan, pitch your book to the media and other markets, talent booking producers, social media and other platforms, create reader engagement and give your book internet presence. Your marketing intern is the key person -- if you're only allowed one intern, this is the one you want. The Computer Science or Graphic Designer student person can serve as your website administer. It's a win-win for everyone.

You do not need to have a large corporate office to secure an intern or team. The college campus, local library or local Starbuck's are great convenient meeting locations to discuss the project. Assign them tasks and have them provide a weekly report with results. With many organizations offering the flexibility to work remotely these days, it'll teach interns to productively work independently and in small groups as well as accountability.

#3 Launch or Re-Launch your Book

Whether your book is an anticipated release, newly released or release five years ago, create an extensive launch or re-launch campaign with strategies and scheduled events along with well thought-out initiatives to increase the sales performance and visibility of you and your book.

Have a launch or re-launch party at unique venues – make it exclusive and a big deal. Inviting the masses sometimes doesn't work. People like to feel important. If they are invited to a private invitation-only event, chances are they'll come. This will also make the individuals who weren't invited want access to your event and your book. People want what they can't have. Suddenly, your book and event invitation are hot commodities that readers want to get their hands on.

Once you increase the distribution channels which will only take a second to do, you can re-launch as it a "National Release" campaign. Give it a catchy theme to attract and excite people about the book. You can also create a new edition: a clean version, a version in Spanish, an audio version, a Christmas edition, a bonus chapter, a new cover. Authors and publishers strategically and creativity do this all the time. Give your book a new angle to attract more readers. Be sure to cross races and genders. Do not put yourself in a box even if your book as a specific theme. Make it appeal to all types and levels.

If your book has been out over a year, re-launch it. This should be #1 on the list but adding more distribution channels comes first!!! Expand your reach!

#4 Learn your Audience

Your marketing intern can help you with this. Research and understand the demographics of your readers, and how to reach your audience based on their consumer behavior. Their consumer behavior and buying patterns tell you all you need to know about your audience. Their social media sites, type of books and magazines they read, radio stations they listen to, where they shop, things they often purchase, their purchasing power and disposable income. Marketing is a large part of psychology and consumer patterns. Interesting! The faster you learn this, the faster you'll reach a larger audience.

If you are not able to get a team or an intern, you can learn the demographics of your audience yourself. Define your audience and most importantly - research, research, research!

Once you have identified your target audience, create a marketing campaign to cost-effectively reach your readers. This is one of the most important components of your building your brand and ultimately your readership. You're probably not going to make millions of dollars, but at least you can reach millions of readers. Your goal is to get as much exposure as you can and have as many people know your name, your brand and your book.

Speak to your audience in their language. Learn what that is, learn what they like, what type of music and radio stations they listen to, what magazines and newspapers they read, what Pandora stations they regularly enjoy, what websites they frequent, and what they "like" or follow on Facebook, Twitter and Instagram. Use this information as a marketing tool to customize your campaign, and reach your audience. It works!

#5 Hire a Publicist

I believe in free help. You can easily get a communications, English or marketing student to fulfill this role. They'll need to be driven to get you and your book in front of as many people. They should also have excellent communications skills, a strong yet friendly presence and be tenacious. They should also have the ability to develop strong relationships and be likeable.

They will not, however, have the same level of fire or passion for your book as you but be sure it's pretty darn close. You want someone who is self-motivated and driven with a strong commitment to excellence.

Have the publicist or intern send a pitch via email to the booking producers of the local media, Good Morning America, the Today Show, Ellen, all the day and late night talk shows, news programs, etc. Start there, create a buzz! Make sure they're relentless but not pushy. Being pushy with a producer will only confirm their reason for denying your request for an interview or story. No means no. Move on the next opportunity, there's plenty out there.

#6 Create an Author Page

Create an Author page on Amazon.com through Amazon's Author Central, it's free. Amazon also helps promote your book. Interestingly, I get emails from Amazon to buy my own book. It's nice to see and a nice way to start my day after checking my early morning emails!

This is a simple process and gives potential readers an opportunity to learn more about you as the author. You can add your bio, professional photo, bibliography, blogs, book trailer, videos, a link to your website as well a real-time newsfeed of your Twitter account.

It's a nice touch to add for free, and increase your credibility and visibility as an author.

#7 Build an Email Distribution List

Create a list of everyone you know and send weekly or bi-weekly updates or teasers about your book to drive them to your website or distribution site to buy the book. Don't overdo it with the emails, the book could lose its value or worse, make people lose interest. Use this strategy just enough to create a buzz. This will also allow you to keep your readers and supporters in the loop. Keep it short and sweet. They don't need a lengthy email, they can buy your book for that.

You can also establish a contract with an email communication company to send vertical emails to your contacts. The company will also report analytics on the performance of your email campaigns. The reports will identify the number of people whom opened, clicked and forwarded your email along with the number of bounce-backs. This is vital information to help you measure the effectiveness and success of each email campaign, and further, will allow you to improve in areas of opportunities.

#8 Create an Interest

Give a few copies of your book away to those who are going to read and promote your book for you. Encourage them to tell others to read it. If they share the book, tell them to only allow their friends to read for the first ten pages. If they want to read more, they'll have to purchase their own. Word-of-mouth is powerful marketing, and free.

#9 Create a Demand

Make people want your book. Whether they read it or not, make them want to get their hands on a copy. You have to make it the hottest thing everyone wants. I created a selfie-craze with readers from across the nation flooding social media with selfies of themselves posing with my book *Disloyalty*. It caught on fire – everyone wanted to get their hands on the book just to post a selfie with the book to post on their social media sites. They created a trend.

I also gave the book to a few people that I knew would create a buzz for me. When they offered to pay me for my book, I told them the only I would like in return was for them to asked post their selfie with the book on their Facebook page and tag me. It's a two-for-one strategy. One post obtains access, at times, to more than two-times the amount of friends. In many cases over 3,000 people would potentially see that one impression which only took a minute to post. Creating this type of catchy phenomenon will create a demand, and the book will sell itself. There is power in numbers, and money!

#10 Invite Website Subscribers

Invite readers to subscribe to your website. Once they've subscribed to your website, add them to your email distribution list. Thank them, keep them in the loop and engaged. Schedule an email communication campaign. Send purposeful, short emails. Again, don't overdo it. It'll lose its value and people will not click on or forward your email. Even worse, they'll unsubscribe or delete the email prior to reading. Be strategic in your messaging and subject line – use key words to entice them to open your email.

#11 Write Articles

Write articles that tie to your book and publish them in the right publications. You can also write and send query letters to editors of magazine publications to write and publish a short story about your book as a freelancer or contributor to their magazine. It'll give you exposure and access to their hundreds of thousands of readers. It's a bit of more work and time consuming to write an explosive story, but certainly worth it. Write one good article or short story, and re-circulate to the hundreds of magazines out there. It's free, you'll get name recognition and exposure – and sell more books.

#12 Create a Social Media Presence

Establish a Facebook page, Instagram page, and Twitter handle for the book as well. Invite all your social media friends, followers and readers to like or follow your page. Post daily or weekly updates about your book, milestones, signings and other events. Continue the buzz surrounding your book. If you haven't already, be sure to create a website for the book; you can set it up to redirect to your main page so you don't have to create new content. It'll contribute to branding the book.

#13 Create Ads on Facebook

Facebook paid ads will increase your engagement and activity with your followers and potential readers. This is a very low cost. I did this for my book, *Disloyalty*, and reached over 9,000 targeted readers within hours for less than $6 per day. You can customize your ads, define your target audience, set the ad frequency, ad positioning, and the type of engagement you're looking for, whether it's for impressions, how many people see your ad in their newsfeed, click for likes, views, etc.

Facebook will give you a daily insight report on the performance of your ads. The report will indicate how many people viewed and clicked on your ad. It's an outstanding tool to gauge potential readership and a tool to help you design subsequent campaigns.

#14 Online Book Give-a-ways

Create contests to give your book away. Be creative. Do it sparingly. After you've created the demand, make them want it more. People are instantaneous, they want things now so create opportunities for them to win a copy today. Post a catchy, fun, simple contest on your official Facebook or Twitter page for people to comment on the contest post, the more comments the more it will appear in the newsfeeds of their friends of friends - that's exponentially increased exposure. More exposure equals increase sales. By the end of the day, select a winner. Post the winners name to your Facebook page, and your other social media pages, and tag the winner. You've just made one person's day, and made hundreds more want your book.

#15 Create a Reader's Guide

You can create a guide with 15-20 thought-provoking questions for your readers to keep them engaged and interested in your book. Use this similar guide for book club discussions and appearances to initiate dialogue. You can also publish this guide in the back of your book or on your website. Your readers will appreciate the guide, and it will provoke their interest more and give them specific to thinks about while connecting to your book, the characters and message of your book.

#16 Host Author Hangouts

You will not be able to physically get in front of all your readers throughout the world but with technology you virtually can. They are many videoconferencing tools and free webcast sites you can join. Schedule a date, promote it, and make it fun. Include a theme, a Q&A, be creative and accessible to your readers. Some website allow you to record the hangout session. For those who were not able to virtually attend the podcast can view it at their convenience. You can post it to your website, Author page or create a DVD for interested readers.

#17 Online Book Discussions

Similar to hosting author hangouts, schedule dates on all social media formats and have a one-hour discussion. Facebook, Twitter, Google+, etc. Promote it the right way, create a buzz and make people want to attend. Establish a hashtag so readers can join the conversation. Make it exciting. Strategically schedule it at a time that majority of your readers are available to participate and join the discussion. Additionally, you can use the reader's guide as a tool to advance the online discussion.

#18 Write a press release

Research sample templates online and create a press release to immediately capture the attention of journalists, anchors and the media. Send it to everyone. Create urgency with it by attaching it to an event you're having or a date when you have something going on. Lack of urgency or an activity date means it's not as important as others, and goes to the back of their pile of press releases and media requests. They'll get to it possibly one day, if at all. If and when they decide to, it may be too late. Be smart.

#19 Guest Blogging

Blogging will give you additional exposure. Have you noticed a common theme in this book so far? It's all about increasing your exposure, and bringing awareness to your brand. You should investigate opportunities by researching online and identifying the best websites and publications to become a guest blogger. Make sure you have a strong marketing campaign built around the guest blogging initiative to entice readers to visit the site to read your blog. You can also create video teasers as well similar to mini-commercials. Create short enticing teasers. Your email distribution list will come in very handy for this purpose.

#20 Get Reviews of Your Book

Entice and encourage your readers to leave reviews about your book on your Amazon site or other distribution website. Reviews help potential readers determine if they should read or purchase your book. Create contests around receiving reviews. Be creative. This component is crucial, and can make or break you as an Author. Once the reviews from readers are posted publically, they cannot be deleted so make sure you are producing quality material. The good news is legitimate readers who purchased your book are listed as such on Amazon.

#21 Get a Literary Agent

This is not really necessary if you build the right team of unpaid interns, or even if you take the time to learn what a literary agent does and do it yourself. The role of an agent is time consuming and intense, and possibly expensive. They make a ton of calls and daily sending emails while working as your advocate to get you in front of as many people. If you have the time, go for it yourself but I would suggest getting an agent if you're not going to be able to give it your all. You'll want to properly represent yourself. First impressions are everything so make it top notch.

#22 Speaking Engagements

You're now an author with credibility. People will love to schedule you to speak on various topics and about your book. Contact libraries, schools, conferences, associations, and literary workshops. You can, of course, sell and sign your book after each engagement. Bring your team of interns with you to manage the sales table, sell books and related products, and to help with crowd management.

#23 Sell your Brand, not the Book

If you effectively promote your brand and your book topic, the book will sell itself. "Buy my book now" campaigns are cheesy, counterproductive and unappealing to readers. These call-to-action strategies usually don't work and make the authors appear desperate. Post a "About the Author" message on your social media page with your bio to gain reader interest. After reading your well-written bio, they should be impressed and have more of an interest in your published work.

#24 Attend and Present at Conferences

Present at conferences or workshops surrounding the topic or idea from your book. Generally after conferences, attendees purchase speaker items. This is another great way to get in front of potential readers, gain exposure, and a get your name and your book out there to the public. You wrote the book, so you're an expert on that particular topic or short story. Many conferences pay a fee to the speakers. This is a great opportunity to increase your income and credibility as an author.

#25 Conduct Workshops

Similar to presenting at conferences, create workshops surrounding the topic of your book, or on how to write a book. If you learned a lesson or simplified process from writing your book, develop a workshop about it. Think of something you're very good at as an author that other people can benefit from. Build it and the people will come. Host the workshops at a local hotel, school, church, as well as webinars.

#26 Create Urgency!!!

Give your readers a reason to want your book now. Give offers with immediate deadlines or expiration dates. If it's too far out, readers will feel they can wait until later to act. If you give them too much times, they'll end up doing something else and forget about your book. Give them an immediate call to action. Create a one- or two-day sale. Announce it the day before to get readers anticipating the sale.

#27 Partner with Other Authors

Partnering with another authors allows the two to collaborate on marketing efforts and events while supporting each other. This will give each of you an advantage and access to additional readers. You can also share an exhibitor booth at book fairs, expos, and other venues to reduce your overhead. You'll be able to split the registration expenses which in the end will make a big difference financially.

I have partnered with two different authors, we've helped promote each other, and attended events together and collaborated on other projects. We each have different target audience, genres, and different styles of writing which makes it very nice. In addition, we share ideas and brainstorm of other ways to support each other. Authors know the struggle book promotions, and often they wouldn't mind the collaboration so network with other authors as much as possible. If nothing else, you can offer each other unique advice.

#28 Partner with Merchants!

Sell your book in book stores and other store merchants. Find ways to partner with the stores. I'm not talking about the normal price split or book consignment but perhaps in running promotions, book signing parties with a theme, wine and cheese socials, an exclusive section of the store or book store, your own author corner. Be creative, think outside the box. It's a win-win for you and the stores.

#29 Schedule Book Readings

This is pretty obvious, or it at least it should be but too often it's not scheduled. Call your local libraries, they have book readings all the time. Get on their calendar, promote the reading on your website, send out short emails to your distribution list, social media, etc.

Book readings are not limited to libraries, you can schedule one with the bookstore where your book is sold. Get in front of as many people as you can. Prior to the reading, select 2-3 passages to read to your guests. People will be in and out during the event, and others may stay the entire time so you will not want to repeatedly read the same excerpts over and over.

#30 Speak in Related Classes

Speak with professors, teachers or department chairs at high schools and colleges to include this as a required reading for courses. Teachers and college instructors generally are required or encouraged to have a guest speaker in their class at least once a semester, so position yourself. Identify the most appropriate class to speak in. Go to the school's website and search through the faculty or teacher directory. For example, you can search for all 12th grade English faculty, or Literature professors. The directory will generally include their email addresses. Send them a short email with "Guest Speaker" in the subject line. Create an interest, a demand and urgency.

Tell them you're going to be in their area speaking in schools during a specific week and you're only available on certain days. They'll love to schedule you. It'll also give them administrative time which they can always use to grade papers, make copies and do other things they usually don't have time for. Start scheduling now.

#31 Create Engagement

Engage with book clubs, school visits, workshops, libraries, writing groups, library readings. Find out who's reading books, and reach out to them to schedule a book discussion, book parties, or just to give them a copy of your book to read and share with others.

Create campaigns to drive readers to your social media pages and website. Continuous engagement will keep readers actively interested and you at the forefront.

#32 Maximize Vacations!

You definitely deserve the getaway and should take the time to recharge and relax. However, you will want to schedule at least one meeting, appearance, book signing or speaking engagement during your vacation. Schedule the event prior to arriving to your travel destination so you can plan on relaxing the rest of your trip. Keep it to a minimum, perhaps an hour or two so you don't overwhelm yourself. You can possibly reserve a hospitality room at the hotel or have an informal book signing and reading at the lobby bar for the hotel guests.

If you are traveling internationally, this opportunity will create international exposure. Give a few copies away to other hotel guests and travelers to spread the word about your book to their network of friends. Also encourage your readers and friends to bring a copy of your book with them on their vacations to read on the

SHARI W. QUINN

beach, and loan to other guests or airplane travelers.

56

#33 Create an url for the Book

If you already have a website, contact your webhost to create a url for the book. You can link the book to your primary web page so you do not have to recreate the content or build an entire new page. Should you ever decide to create content for the page, the url is already yours and you don't have to worry about someone buying the url address. My url for my book *Disloyalty* is disloyalythebook.com and is immediately forwarded to shariquinn.com

#34 Create a Book Trailer

This is not as hard or expensive as it sounds. You can connect with an filmmaker or editing student or graphic editor to produce this for you, or you can do it yourself – free of charge. Use your resources and YouTube. There are a ton of software applications and resources out there that can help you create this. If done correctly, it'll look like you paid thousands of dollars for it. I created my own book trailer and viewers thought a high-paid Hollywood movie producer created it. If you put enough time into it, it'll enhance the quality and add credibility to your book. Give it a try.

#35 Donate Books

Donate a few copies to local libraries, hair salons, schools, dentist office, doctor's office, teachers, book club leaders, co-workers, book reviewers, etc. Think of high traffic locations with waiting rooms, busy lobbies or a place that is frequently visited by customers that can enjoy your book while waiting. Chances are they will not finish the book during their wait; and the intrigue of your book will prompt to them to purchase it and tell others.

If your book would appeal to a specific type of readers, groups, leaders, give it to them as well. Think of a comfortable number of books to donate. You may actually find yourself giving a few more than you expected which is OK because you will reap what you sow. Donating books is the same as planting seeds and sowing, you will reap the benefits of book sales in the future.

The point of donating your book is to gain as much interest and exposure as possible.

#36 Start a 501c3 Organization

If your book centers around a particular issue or cause, you can start a not-for-profit organization around the issue. The grant writers you earlier gave your book copies to, as suggested earlier, can help identify and write eligible grants to support and address the issue, as well as help the population you're serving. Once you get the grant, you can create a line item to allocate consultant fees to the grant writer; or you can add another intern to your team. You can select a public administration major – they usually take not-for-profit and grant writing courses. If not contact the department chair for these courses to find a strong student.

#37 Alumni Newsletter

Put an announcement in your alumni newsletter for word of mouth with your high school, undergrad and graduate schools. Alumni almost always support their fellow alums. The schools love to support their alums as well. Send your college alumni office an email, a press release or call them to let them know the brief details of your new book along with a picture of your book cover. They'll be happy to let other alums and staff know about your accomplishment, and they'll be happy to share your great news in the newsletter. Often potential students of the college read the newsletter and it'll be nice to read your success story from the future alma mater. This alumni newsletter announcement will increase your exposure and readership nationwide particularly since alums live everywhere across the country and internationally. Further, plan a book signing at your alma mater school library or book store.

#38 Schedule Radio Interviews

Have your publicist or intern take care of this for you. Sometimes radio stations will want you to place a radio commercial for your book to schedule in pre-recorded interviews. It's rare that they'll schedule an on-air interview but it's will not hurt to ask. From a business perspective, I understand it but try to bypass the advertising executive to talk with the program director or music director. Sometimes you can speak with the radio personality whom has a live show, they may be willing to have you on their show as a guest. Perhaps talk to the show host or radio personality to advocate for you. It's worth a shot.

#39 Create a Checklist

Using a spreadsheet or word processing software, create a checklist with each item from this list. Set a realistic deadline for each item and timely check off each item off the list.

Print the list and keep it visible where you can see it and refer to it daily. As mentioned, it's easy to set distracted so the visual of the checklist should help you stay on task. Reward yourself when you have completed the checklist, or after every milestone. It'll give you something to look forward to and show you that you are closer to achieving your goal.

#40 Always Seek New Opportunities

Always seek new opportunities to promote your book. I have only listed a fraction of several book marketing and promotion opportunities. Whenever you meet someone, there's an opportunity; whenever you go somewhere, there's an opportunity. Sometimes the opportunity will not fall on your lap or be as obvious, you'll have to pay attention and connect the dots when you potential opportunities surface.

In your quest for new opportunities, be genuine – not greedy. Real recognizes real, and people buy from people they like. They do not like fake people so be genuine. It'll go a long way.

#41 Stay Focused

It is very easy to get distracted. Keep your eyes on the prize, and on your checklist. Minimize your distractions and stay focused. Sometimes to elevate you have to separate yourself from a few people and refrain from the usual outings for a while. It's short-term so don't worry. Your hard work and focus will pay off in the end. You can treat yourself later – and with your royalties.

#42 Thank your Readers!

Always thank your readers and supporters. Use your email distribution list to send them a simple quick thank you, holiday greetings, etc. Acknowledge them individually or collectively on social media: your Facebook page with their name in the tag, along with Twitter or Instagram. Even though times have changed, a nice handwritten thank-you in the mail is a nice gesture people appreciate. Your supporters will feel appreciated that you took the time to handwrite them a personalized thank you card.

You can also plan an appreciation party or social on the anniversary of your release or at the milestone mark of your book – maybe when it sold a certain number of copies, or became a best seller. You can pick the milestone or purpose for the celebration but certainly celebrate your success, your readers and your supporters, they are the reason you reached the top! You didn't make it this far on your own.

At your appreciation party, you can sell more books, a new edition or announce your next project. Or perhaps not at all. Perhaps you'll just want to enjoy the moment and celebrate with your supporters – but whatever you do, thank them!

SHARI W. QUINN

About the Author

Shari W. Quinn, owner of Shari Quinn Publishing, best-selling author of *Disloyalty*, and NBC affiliate WNYT's Channel 13's *Today's Woman,* is a native of Albany, New York. After living in suburban Atlanta for eight years, she relocated back to New York's Capital Region. She is a leader in education, a college instructor, and has been in the higher education industry for more than 15 years. She has served as a guest speaker in over 75 high schools throughout New York State.

She earned her Master's degree in Business Administration (MBA) with a concentration in Marketing from the University of Phoenix in Atlanta; a Bachelor's in Marketing and Management from Siena College in Loudonville, NY; and an Associate's degree in Liberal Arts from Hudson Valley Community College in Troy, NY. She has completed more than two years toward her Doctor of Education (Ed.D.) degree in Educational Leadership and currently pursuing her doctorate's in Education with Northeastern University in Boston.

She is the proud mother of three children, Sharia, Ruffus "Pop" IV, and Malik; has two beautiful grandchildren, Anthony Jr., and DeShari'ay; and lives in upstate New York.

SHARI W. QUINN

www.ingramcontent.com/pod-product-compliance
Lightning Source LLC
Chambersburg PA
CBHW032015190326
41520CB00007B/487